THANK YOU VETERANS

MY FIRST VETERANS DAY

WHAT IS VETERANS DAY ??

Veterans Day is a U.S. holiday observed on November 11 th each year to honor military veterans who have served in the U.S. Armed Forces. It celebrates their service and sacrifices in protecting the nation. It originally marked the end of World War I but now honors all veterans

Sammy was excited because today was Veterans Day, and he was going to celebrate it for the first time with his father. His dad was a veteran, and Sammy couldn't wait to wear his special costume that looked just like his dad's old uniform. His mom had even helped him pin a pretend medal on his shirt. He felt like a real soldier!

Sammy and his father got ready to head to the town's Veterans Day parade. "Dad, what does Veterans Day mean?" Sammy asked. His dad smiled and said, "It's a day to honor all the men and women who served in the military to protect our country, just like I did." Sammy nodded, excited to learn more.

Before leaving, Sammy's father gave him a small American flag to wave during the parade. "Hold this proudly, son. It stands for everything we protect as soldiers." Sammy clutched the flag tightly, determined to honor all the veterans just like his dad.

THE VETERANS DAY PARADE

The streets were lined with people waving flags as the Veterans Day parade began. Sammy could see soldiers marching, veterans riding in decorated cars, and even a big marching band playing patriotic songs. His dad waved at his fellow veterans as they passed by, and Sammy waved his flag high in the air.

Sammy's dad pointed to a group of older veterans walking slowly together. "Those men served a long time ago. Some of them fought in wars before I was even born," he said. Sammy looked in awe. He didn't realize there were veterans from so many different times. "They're all heroes, right?" he asked. "Absolutely," his dad replied.

As the parade continued, Sammy saw a group of women veterans walking together. "Women can be veterans too?" Sammy asked, surprised. His dad nodded. "Yes, women serve in the military too, and they are just as brave and strong." Sammy smiled, learning something new about what it meant to be a hero.

LEARNING ABOUT VETERANS

After the parade, Sammy and his dad went to the town's Veterans Memorial Park. They walked by large statues and plaques with the names of loca heroes. Sammy's dad explained that these were people who had served their country and some had given their lives to protect others. Sammy felt proud to be there with his dad.

Sammy's dad knelt beside one of the plaques and pointed out a name. "This is my friend who I served with in the military," he said softly. "He was brave, and today we remember and honor him." Sammy looked at the name and felt a mix of sadness and pride, realizing how important it was to remember the people who had done such important things.

As they continued walking, Sammy asked his dad, "Does being a soldier mean being away from home a lot?" His dad nodded. "Yes, sometimes it does. We miss our families, but we do it because we love our country." Sammy hugged his dad, feeling proud but also glad his father was home with him now.

SAYING THANK YOU

When they got home, Sammy had an idea. "Dad, can I draw a picture of us together in our uniforms to thank you for being my hero?" His dad smiled, feeling touched. "That's a great idea, Sammy. I would love that," he said, watching Sammy rush off to gather his crayons and paper.

Sammy spent the afternoon drawing a picture of him and his dad standing side by side, both wearing their uniforms and holding flags. When he was done, he showed it to his dad, who smiled proudly. "This is perfect, Sammy. I'll keep it forever," his dad said, hanging it up on the refrigerator for everyone to see.

That evening, as they sat down for dinner, Sammy looked at his dad and said, "Thanks for teaching me about Veterans Day, Dad. I'm really proud of you." His dad smiled, his eyes full of love. "Thank you, Sammy. I'm proud of you too, and I'm glad we could celebrate together." Veterans Day had become a special memory for them both.

QUIZ

Circle the correct answer

1. What did the child in the story dream of becoming?

a) A firefighter

b) A police officer

c) A doctor

Who showed the children around the police station?

a) Officer Carla

b) Officer Mike

c) Officer Jane

What color vest did the child wear as part of the school safety patrol?

a) Red

b) Yellow

c) Green

What did the child dream of doing when they became a police officer?

a) Driving a police car and waving at kids

b) Climbing a tall building

c) Flying a helicopter

Made in the USA
Las Vegas, NV
05 November 2024

11176198R00021